The
Lady Rose
Report

ALSO BY SIERRA NELSON

In Case of Loss

I Take Back the Sponge Cake

The Lachrymose Report

Sierra Nelson

POETRY
NORTHWEST
EDITIONS

Everett • Seattle
Washington

lachrymose
(from Latin lacrimōsus, *from* lacrima *a tear):*
given to shedding tears readily; tearful.

sunt lacrimae rerum et mentem mortalia tangunt
there are tears of (or for) things and mortal things touch the mind
—Virgil, *The Aeneid*, Book I, line 462

see also
lacrimal lake:
the small cistern-like area of the conjunctiva at the medial angle of
the eye, in which the tears collect after bathing the front surface of
the eyeball and the conjunctival sac.

Cover art: Sally Warring (pondlifepondlife.com)
Book design: Christian Larson

Poetry NW Editions is an independent, non-profit educational press
in residence at Everett Community College.

LIBRARY OF CONGRESS CONTROL NUMBER: 2018944212
Names: Nelson, Sierra, author
Title: The Lachrymose Report / Sierra Nelson
Description: First Edition / Everett, Washington: Poetry NW Editions, 2018
ISBN-13: 978-1-949166-00-2 (hardcover)

Possession Sound Poetry Series Volume 1
Produced with the generous support of The Kinsman Foundation

Poetry NW Editions
2000 Tower Street
Everett, Washington 98201

www.poetrynw.org

TABLE OF CONTENTS

The
Lachrymose
Report

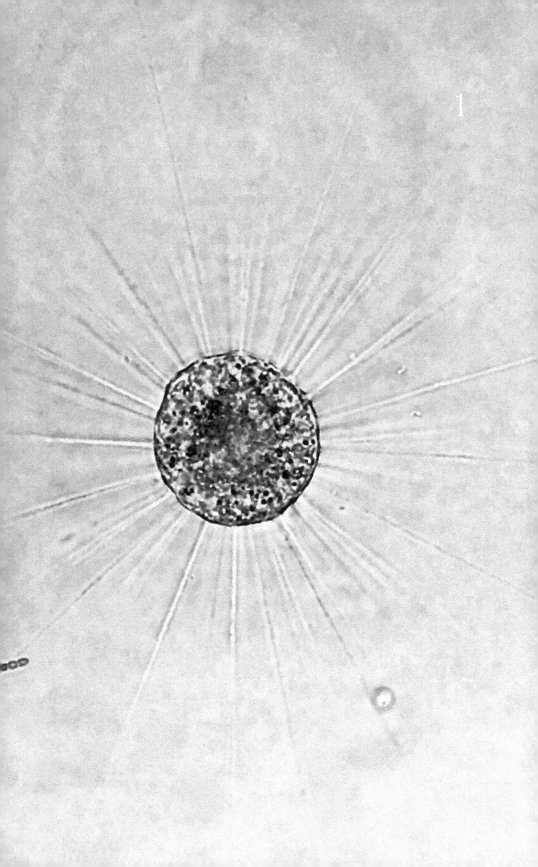

YOUR EYES ARE CLOSED BUT YOU
AREN'T DREAMING

You are traveling slowly,
like a great shipwreck still sailing.
Almost tenderly, the sun puts a hand to your forehead.
Yes, you think, I've been unwell. You sink into the feeling.
But the sun is blind and must touch everything:
always feeling its gold way forward towards the dark.

ROGUE WAVE

A rogue wave of old grief capsized me at the bar.

The night in my mouth had the names all wrong:
Herodotus.   Herodotus.

My chair was upside down
but I was making it look casual.

Earlier, when my glasses flew off and his glasses flew off
and they did a little orbit around each other
before returning to our faces —
but that was before Herodotus.

Herodotus tells us:
Human happiness never continues long in one stay.

I report my old love in longhand.
I report old grief in perfect sobbing penmanship.
I report my flight from the bar as a series of not-falling,
bat-wing-like movements.

Logographers, I need you! Graffiti artists, I need you!
Dancing man at the bus stop, I need you!

I have staggered free of the wreck of one year,
I can surely come clear of another.

NOT TOWARDS A REAL, TOWARDS ANOTHER

In order to begin the adventure I must first tell you that there will be no adventure.
Nobody wanted gingernut. Through discontinuity there will be continuity.
If her eyes are opened or closed, does it matter? Blood leaves. Remnants
of the government. I live here, where else would I want to live? How lost
you looked without your glasses. Cake crumbs were going fast but the oatmeal
wasn't popular. Melancholy represents a capacity for infinite feeling. What the hell
were you thinking? All night long the sounds of doors and keys.
Dear Peter, busses are always delayed and I'm drunk again. Isolation occurred
amidst myriad isolations. The moon came in through the slats. Her mates
were touching her with their antennae as if puzzled by such crazy behavior.
Singing: *Yer gonna lose a good thing*. At times a certain feeling hangs
weights upon me, like madstones. Girl in a soft pink hat. Someone
has found the buttons and mice with crystal-studded collars.
The last word on page 129, which is missing, is
        . There will be a small death in this poem.
hello.
Dear sir: I regret to inform you that I did not find you at the bottom of my soup.
Sad-eyed 1939. We didn't know where we were. Thank goodness we saw you.
Had to – what was he up to – laughed outright. One false step and it's bye-bye Raoul.
The twig caterpillar deceives the moth. Dear Gregory, in the other part of my dream.
This time he hoped for a chance to see more but did not after all. Not attached
to any specific existence, not attached to life. You beautiful kiddo.
And the blossom beetles bore us bravely, though we were heavy with jam.

POSTCARD (ALMOST BREAKFAST ANYTIME)

You said, "It makes you wonder,"
And I knew just what you meant.
The waitress had a shiner.
You had one more cigarette.

Someone said, "In Wichita,"
And the guy in the kitchen laughed.
The toast had extra butter.
I stacked the half-n-halfs.

Plate of pancakes, plate of eggs,
Water, coffee, poured in rounds.
You had a watch but we'd lost track —
"Why don't we skip town?"

But we did nothing of the kind.
Cherry. Jelly. Valentine.

FOR LRRH

1.

Little was given. Red was given.
Girl so given as to be unsaid.
Riding was said but not given.
Cheeks were given to crimson
beneath a hood: hood was given.

Flowers convincing as wolves were gathered.
The first choice, a good one, was bad.
To stray. She does stray.
A small foot given to a meadow.
Shadows gathered in pools of delay.

2.

A wolf's mouth may be red, but
Red is not a wolf.

Apple is not a wolf.
Cloak is not a wolf.
Enchanted gold-red hair is not a wolf.

The best part of me
is swinging an axe, whistling
through the dapple.

Undeniable wetting of teeth.

3.

My life, what big eyes!
(The better to eat you with.)

Then her belly filled with stones,
thread tugged through heavy fur.

HANDLE ONLY IN DARKNESS
OR IN A RED SAFELIGHT

Handle only in darkness or in a red safelight,
like a heartbeat. A yellow film can be attached
to deepen the contrast. *Dormir,* to sleep,
as in the dormouse, asleep for ¾ of its life.
It is not a waste to sleep so much,
nor is it a waste to think of you so much,
thoughts spreading beaver tail,
my rudder and alarm.
Serefe! to drink with one's honor.
There is no need to draw a knife.
Watch the film develop before plunging it in stop.
Lykke, the Danish happiness,
usually sold in extremely long lengths,
we rarely have on hand.
We place the internegative
on a wooden frame,
photograph it on low speed,
blue-sensitive film.
It is true we kissed once
when we shouldn't have,
under a 100-watt tungsten light bulb.
Now leap dramatically
out of the burrow, to avoid
any predators skulking around.

SELF-SONG OF THE LITTLE JUG

My life began with a foot
which felt the earth turn beneath it
in keeping with the stars.

Where my mind pushed out
against the air in wet despair
I became bellow, breath,
bend, breadth — I learned
to hold, carry.

My shoulders rise from the pool
like a dreamer from philosophy.
I narrow where I sing, I swallow.
I turn my lips out to kiss
and my first kiss was fire.

I skim the rim of thirst's circumference.

WE TAKE THE FUNICULAR

Giddy on major life decisions
averted — free! — we take
the funicular up the mountain.
Is this the Italian hill-town
famous for its boars?

"On my left shoulder, you will see
a beautiful cloud," a tour guide says.
Rice in the cobblestones,
we stand before the gothic sunlight
and squint into the molten gilding.

We are paying for last night's
good dancing in bad shoes.
In shady corners,
teenagers make out with jaded abandon
and we suppress thoughts of afternoons
and earlobes, speak casually of
the wine of the region, admire
the tufa.

I long for a home where I could
use this giant platter
painted with lemons —
to present to you a fish
wrapped up in paper
like a bouquet.

Maybe you could learn to play
the accordion from that boy
who only knows one song
but plays it very well.

The city gets sleepy and closes
all its shutters,
except for the underground tour
of medieval pigeon coops.
We'll take it!
Our guide directs,
"If you look just under your head,
you should see a little
passage of steps."

The sun is flirtatiously
slouching toward the horizon.

Be sure not to miss
the last train back
to the life you thought you wanted.

GET THE GODS ON THE AEROPHONE

From atop this aerie we see the masses
flick on and off their small light switches.
It's no use, kid.
Down the breakneck highlands
we'll send our horses, by and by,
and all the clouds stutter something we longed to say.

Beat it.
Go on and scram.
It's time you lost your downy feathers,
showed a little pluck,
beyond the meadows and the brouhaha of May.
Haven't you sensed it all along?
Only someone else can read your face,
and there's just no way of telling.
But I'll tell you, my friend —
there was a time when laughter was the thing.
Shepherds, why this joyous strain,
folded hands and tufts of angel wing?
I don't know why, but you just took to it.

This just in: gale warnings and a small craft advisory.

DESTRUCTION ISLAND COULD BE SEEN
IN THE DISTANCE

For one whole life I mistook love for surprise and sadness,
which according to Plutchik's wheel of human emotions
equals disappointment.
Destruction Island could be seen in the distance,
past two seagulls facing opposite directions
I placed prominently so you can see them
when you enter my home.
In Turkey, a wedding couple exchange wreaths with their vows —
a wreath of flowers for the bride, a wreath of grapes for the groom.
In fireworks, stars are specially arranged so as to create a shape.
In Georgia O'Keefe, a color that could say more than words,
as in a pelvis bone held against the sky.
My love, for so long I thought love was simply
a room free from remorse and with running water.
And now the joy of astonishment looking into your eyes —
a splendid restaurant for men and women.
And now the trust — modern, fireproof —
of light pouring in through your kitchen window.

NOCTURNE

A well opens its mouth to drink the moon
not realizing it's the moon that wants a drink.
Thirst is different at night.
Tall stalks complain in pained whispers
of their sciatica,
not realizing that nerve
is just spring
trying to shoot through them.

A truck of light fixtures arrives before midnight –
the lamps in their boxes are bundled inside.
A worker shares his cure for eczema
while the driver kicks sleep out of her feet.
An inequality of dreams enters the neighborhood
but has no bearing on who will remember what.

The dew descends in a morbid humor,
unnoticed by the plants and lovers
on which it falls.

WE'LL ALWAYS HAVE CARTHAGE

The head must bow to the heart,
which is why I always look down;
if the earth is round and round
I'll be wrong until the ends of it.

Beautiful, you said, and meant
the sea. Reminding me –
there are walls to be built,
rocks carried.

Now I can't meet you
or your eyes – just the boats
below in the harbor,
burning.

The wind shakes the earth
from its four corners;
the flames are picking up,
or is that me shaking?

Look, I'm right – the sun is
underwater. Now get out of here
with that lion's skin
on your back.

VENUS FOUNTAIN

Just as eye calls to eye
to overlap vision, so the gods
of each fountain niche
deepen the picture.

Look to the center.
Aphrodite is no longer there
pouring water from a vase.

And now the small statues
are gone too — each recess
grown dark and slick,
bubbling over.

    Think of the last time you saw her.

The mind is a naturally dry place,
a desert you carry, full of walls
longing to be loosened.

At the back of the fountain
her last words painted red on stone:

    There is no one for anyone.

Close your eyes.
She left with the sound of water.
You can almost see her —
a pale dress of summer green,
her wet footsteps refreshing
the mosaics, blue flowers falling
from the portico.

LOST & FOUND

Lost my needle of silver, my earring, my compass
slipped off by the pickpocket moon.

Found your two books at the bookstore: "Defamiliarize yourself.
Mr. Patterson yelling." "Like Odysseus?" "No, like his dog."

Lost the free ride zone on the downtown bus, and the homeless man's
sister in Mississippi, the psychoanalyst.

Found my smile that reminded him of her.

Lost the moment the words left my mouth
and unfurled their small metal barbs.

"You lost your mustache," said the man to the waitress,
who laughed.

Found *Whole Lotta Love* on the jukebox.

Found nachos.

Found Wittgenstein, his lost cabin on the mountain,
his solace of shame chopping wood.

Found Kierkegaard and his encouragement:
"Sleeping is the height of genius."

Lost that library book on Black Death
I used to research a paper in 1993.

Found the memory of it, and the fact that as the plague raged on
women's hems rose.

Lost that apartment in New York
and belief in true love.

Found a new love theory involving burnt toast
and spatial perspicacity.

Found *Just My Imagination* on the jukebox
with a skip in it.

Found a renewed interest in drinking
every day.

Lost sense of bare minimum
to feel O.K.

Found *Under Pressure* on the jukebox.

Lost that feeling we had on the long sad drive
to the airport.

Found the woman who found the man
who loves Van Halen almost as much as she does.

Found more whiskey.

Found more stomachache.

Lost the shipwreck with the steel heart,
the fires on the deck.

Found again my name called by an unseen voice.

Lost my student who got up from her hospital bed to dance
just days before she died.

Lost the anchor of two years and a half.

Lost the sorrow that crumpled me to the floor inside my door.

Found a room painted green, one window of blinds
and two beer cans, one window blind with rhododendrons.

Lost my allergy medicine my box of cleaning supplies.

Found my box of underwear.

Found the letter we wrote together to my grandmother.

Lost you.

Found you, and you.

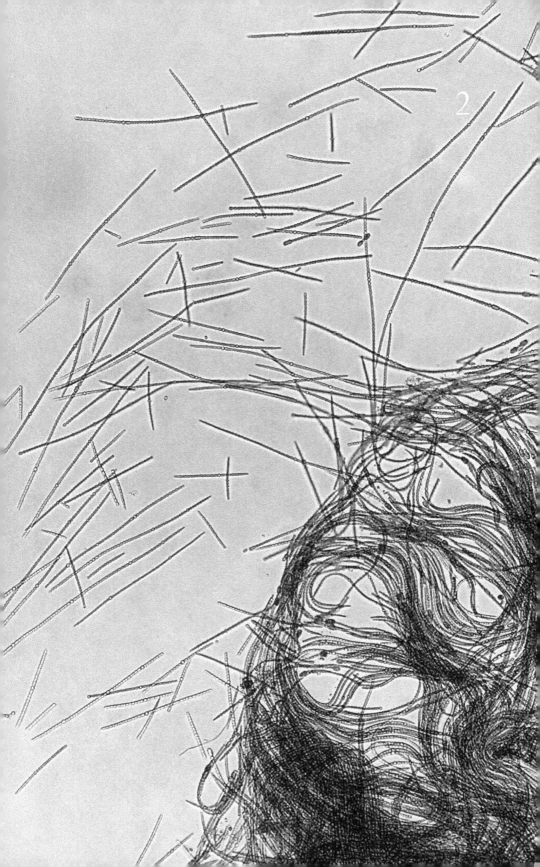

EVERYMAN AND HER CHORUS

Are you happy my friend?
    No I am sorrow.

Is it pale as grass?
    Pale as ashes now.

Is it moon gleams in water?
    No, cold stirring fish scales.

Have you gathered your seeds?
    They are dried ink on old string.

Have you opened the gate yet?
    It was left open for years.

Have you found a light to see by?
    Dark as purpose only.

Is there a star in the well?
    Just a crystal in mud.

Have you come by a hope?
    I have harrowed it to nothing.

What can empty hands give you?
    Warm your fists in your coats.

THE FIRST PHOTOGRAPH

— after Joseph Nicéphore Niépce, "View from the Window at Le Gras"

Perihelion, closest to the sun. Heliography, the image.
Hasn't there been a moment you never wanted to leave?
An outward listlessness, but inwardly lit, light-sensitive?

Previous tests revealed how a feeling, made
transparent, could be transferred to stones.
Hold still, we said to the trees, the slanting rooftops.
Uncap the lens and we are in France.

Through the pinprick it all came to us,
how close we were, upside down,
several hours on the windowsill.
We were surfaces arranged to receive.

The pewter plate revealed buildings turning into salt,
sliding away from themselves,
what we could see but did not know,
the graininess of the shadows.

Later we passed through many hands,
centuries.
We had to leave.

Yet I capture you. Close to the sun.
I coated my longing in bitumen.

RULES FOR WATER

Every few miles a hawk sits on a line, a comma
in landscape. The conversation, mostly silent, threads
along the road: through fields, then coastal.
Where do you think you are going to, going to? See the great

chemicals stream over from the factory,
creepy love letters on diligent currents, as the orange-pink
prink of sunrise lifts smoke-stack plumes.

We have arrived like storm-waves, filled with sticks and stones.
Conduire, to drive, to conduct ourselves, how do we – from here to there,
electricity through water, sensing through saline. You never call me honey
unless something is wrong. But the radio is on. Three great waves,
then a lesser run, then three more.

THE STORY

You're telling that story again, the one in which your mother
believes your college boyfriend visiting you from New York
stole her silver and asks him to take a lie detector test
which escalates to her throwing him out of her house
but also buying him a plane ticket to New York, which he uses,
but delays the departure to try to salvage the romance,
so you go to Vancouver without telling anyone
at which point your entire family believes
you have run away with an outlaw.

For outlaw read husband; for family read forest; without telling in an envelope.
For romance read anger; for plane ticket, resentment; Vancouver is year after year.
For throwing out of the house read a cracked mirror; for lie detector, a glass key.
For silver read virginity; your mother believes your childhood.
Your college boyfriend becomes you on a train
from New York City to Poughkeepsie,
looking to reverse the summer.

Your childhood looks for your virginity.
A glass key escalates to a cracked mirror
and resentment, which he uses.
Anger year after year in an envelope.
The forest believes you have run away with a husband.

EYEGLASSES FOR INSOMNIACS,
OR TESTS OF MENTALITY, READINESS, AND ACHIEVEMENT

I had 15 marbles and lost six.

Write me a letter which says,
I admirred the wintir dresing evry brige with snoe.

Tell the opposite of swan.
If I should say dark, you would say what?

One of the loveliest gifts we received was
night eggs through sugar wrapper.

The year 1600 saw the invention of the wind chariot.
In 1967, eyeglasses for insomniacs.

Would you answer yes or no?

Pascal deduced pressure applied to any one point
of an incomprehensible liquid
creates the sensation
of love transmitted
without loss
to all parts of the liquid.

What's the thing to do if you are lost?

DETECTAPHONE

A person in a red coat (me) picks up the detectaphone
and listens in on the winter morning. Sounds like
air turning into snow but not landing.

A brilliant strategist,
the sun takes a worm's-eye view
of the pine needles,
gets down on their level.

So much importance placed on how
things fall, this one against that,
and call it love, or fate, or
majoritarianism.

The sunlight falls, but everywhere at once.

I fell in my family's foyer,
my wine and a potted plant down with me,
everywhere at once.

The sun holds the hand of a pine needle.

"You're fine, you're fine, we've
called an ambulance."

I quietly replace the receiver.

PICKUP TRUCK PANTOUM

Across the pickup's back bumper, a figure slung
sideways, wrapped and roped in tarp.
Startled is not the right word. It took me a long time
to see that there were antlers,

sideways, sticking out from the roped tarp
wrapped to accentuate girlish curves.
To see that there were antlers
did not dispel my first belief:

a girl's curved body, laying there:
an antlered girl laid low.
Belief's first grief lingers
and even if mistaken, isn't wrong:

an antlered girl: not buck, not deer,
that once lipped berries tenderly from between thorns,
and even if mistaken, isn't wrong,
flicking an ear back at a twig crack of danger.

Lipping berries tenderly from thorns,
and the fragrant green flavor of the neighbor's prized roses,
flicking an ear back at a twig crack of danger:
why run? Lost in her own thoughts.

Roses. The tarp was white. The light changing.
Across the pickup's bumper, a figure slung
and moving forward now, starting to pull away.
Startled is not the right word. It took me a long time.

NOCTURNE

There is a sound of an animal crunching in the other room
but it is the dishwashing machine ratcheting the minutes.

One blip is zip.
I don't really believe that
but now I lay me
head down on the floor.

Nothing can repeat.
Speak to another person.

Now you're somebody else,
take off your glasses.
Now you're somebody else in the rain.
Now I let you be somebody else
in a jacket.
So many things that have happened
have never happened
because I never told anyone.

The crowded white hallway, bells ringing,
wrong wrong wrong wrong wrong.
The transatlantic phone line is faulty.
Jxt'xxmx. What did you say?

Nous nous aimons,
said the ghost
before my head slipped
like a balloon from its fingers.

FOUR METHODS OF SPEAKING

1.

I peeled the apple to the apple core.
I listened and I laughed.

I tore each letter out
until it stood alone.

I did not answer
the blue telephone
until I liked the sound of it.

I never waited for myself
in the mirror — captured
and exhibited.

2.

We arranged the question marks
like a bouquet to catch the light.

This went on for 20 years,
or one year repeated 20 times.

The typewriter keys hit the pages
too softly —

We were outlined in chalk,
but we kept moving.

3.

With firmness of lip and will of the chin
I will try harder.
I stare at the tact of your hairline,
the force of your nose,
the energy of your earlobe.

I am wearing a pink T-shirt
that says INHIBITION.
You are a spectacle, you say,
swilling invitation
in a glass.

Somewhere stick figures lie on a beach —
or sit up, lose a Frisbee, stroll along
or almost drown.
A stick dog swims after a stick.

I place my hand
on your vital temple.

4.

The city was in black & white
except for the moon.

This was the last
of our pen and ink blind portraits,
the word daydreams falling up the page.

Does this song illustrate the architecture?

I was falling asleep
curled up in the chair.

DEAR SIR OR MADAM

You should always end *Yours faithfully* if you do not know the name of the one you are addressing. Before Adam could name the animals, he was not theirs *Sincerely*. He could not be. He was forced to address them formally, *Dear Sir or Madam*, or sometimes, simply: *To Whom It May Concern*. Bowing between man and beast was more common then. As were SASE. The lower ranks of angels were all excellent typists. Look closely at the budding branch, between skin and fur, and you may still see their initials in lowercase (though frequently mistaken for holy signature, or divinatory Encl.). Once Mr. Lamb could lay with Mrs. Lion in *Kind regards*, and *Faithfully*, before they had names to call each other, before others had names to call them.

POSTCARD (GHOST MEAT)

The ghost meat of all the barbeques
we didn't go to haunts our days,
trails us on the train,
hangs around like a smoky weight
in our bellies.

Once I made you a soup
which could never be replicated.
It was made of the ends of everything,
some of it fresh and some of it very old.
Olives were a surprise ingredient.
Every bite was like saying you wished you could stay
and meaning it. The spoon made a satisfying sound
against the ceramic bowl.
There was nothing sorry about that soup.

CYANOBACTERIA AND THE UNDERWORLD

1. *Field Notes*

The cyanobacteria are stressed:
the light of my microscope
too strange, too bright.
In the pond at night
the many are one,
but in the heat they jettison
to individual pips again,
blue-green and swimming freely
toward better, hopeful climes.

In the underworld, Persephone
sends six pomegranate seeds
to hell, and herself after.
In red darkness she breathes
anaerobically, wholly herself
though her life halved.

Meanwhile cyanobacteria, lonely, leaving,
oxygenate, they can't even help it:
make a blue-green heaven
for me that has harrowed them.

2. *Postcard from Persephone*

Through the breach, they heard the waters pour as mountain torrents down a flume,
so sudden change can shudder a person, wear out her wet ropes.
There is no room
to breathe here, though the air smacks of brine and hope.

The breach of the mountain, the scrape of the hull,
the seed husk burst and all her sailors shucked,
the body listing badly: but the skull
hides its hell well, with luck,

while the iron of blood clangs its day after day.
Naught's an obstacle, naught's an angle to the iron way.

3. *It Is Still a Beautiful Dream: Translations Under the Microscope*

hatching, brooding
    put on the boot
metal coffin
    the pair of you
houses on fire
    leaden cloud
swollen eye
    a rest cure
strained peas
    coupon sheet
gift of books
    chimney corner
lackluster eyes
    gather strawberries
become sodden
    stench of gutters
kick in the pants
    stand off and on
sail out for somewhere

at daggers drown
    lead a dance
cuts no ice
    a divided choir
gooseberry fool
    a shaving mirror
tale of a tub
    a heap of stones
speeding up of machines
    a cubby hole
unfrequented street
    caraway seed
a drop too much
    scalding tears
hardly a mouthful
    taken with a spoon
the cupping glass
    lesson learnt by heart
    bitter salt

LET A LITTLE LIGHT IN

1.

From Nero's hot ashes
devils in the guise of crows
rose into a walnut tree.

How well the crusades are going.
How fast the wild horses
are coursing our streets.
Stop them with a white sheet
pulled taut like a snapping sail.

With so many bones
and martyrs' belongings,
we'll be building these churches
for thousands of years.

Erect one now.

The crows laugh
in the backs of their throats.
The bones kneel and pray:
some of them still with wings.

2.

Across your stretched life,
paint the black on thick, then
let a little light in.

With its shying white hoof
and blinding white shoulder,
vision nearly trampled a soldier,
making the feather of his helmet fall.

All your life you've had a dark name.
You've been too long reading
into the night.

For you, the moment will descend
like a beautiful boy's face
on velvet bat wings.

Your pen will lift itself
off the page, your hand with it,
and into the dark you'll follow

your new name pounding
the cobbled streets,
fireworks sparking at its heels.

HOW TO REMEMBER

Heat is invisible but rises,
like the memory of a tree
streams off the orange
you hold in your hand.

That orange was true
as a photograph —
it really happened.
(Remember?)

I believe in love
and the way it leaves you —
a particle and a wave —
until the source is gone
and you're out like a light.

Goodnight. Turn to the cool
outer edge of the sheet.
The ceiling heat stroked
by the sleepy fan.
The smell of orange blossoms
thickening the dark.

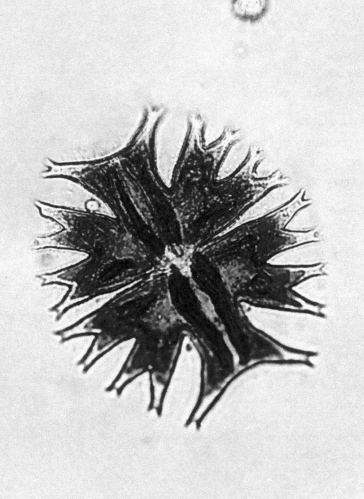

THE LACHRYMOSE REPORT

The city cries
over milk
in the gutter.

Jellyfish gowns
enter the park
and totally crack up
the weeping cherry tree.

All over the world
windows continue to cry,
but it takes centuries
to be registered –

While the sun,
the big faker,
cries in goldfinches.

In the trees
the birds are crying,
but it sounds like
a pretty good
theory on love, actually.

Big whiskey tears
stain everything gold.

Hold me
like a sobbing sunbeam,
please.

Thank you for your
renewed subscription.

SIGNS

When you hear a voice —
low, unexpected,
close to your ear —
and it coils in deep
like a snail into its shell —

don't listen.

It only takes a breeze
to undo a poppy.

Honeysuckle takes
over the air;
black ants spill out from
a crack in the ground,
form a slender ribbon
curving up the rock wall.

Inside, you try to
hold a longing closed —
but the pod's begun to split —
silken seeds can feel the air.

Don't worry. The tunnel
is not as dark as it seems.

That person coming towards you
isn't you.

WE ALL LOVE A LITTLE RUIN

We wanted to go to the underworld!
But all we could find were
bright, bright ruins
and heat-blown poppies.

As fast as we could we ran
under arches, past half-cracked portals –
but never a door dark enough to enter,
steps sensitive enough
to carry us down.

Lizards and small birds flitting
in and out of holes in
crumbling walls.

What did we know of crumbling?

You took one square rock
of me, removed it from
its niche, and leaned
in close to feel
the cool, dark
air inside.

AND YOU WILL KNOW DESIRE BY THE VISION OF THE BEES

— after Karl von Frisch, Bees: Their Vision, Chemical Senses, and Language

1.

Bees love to see blue-green: a color for them more distinct than other hues. (For example, the difference between orange and yellow may cause one backward buzz of hesitation, but a prize of orange or yellow is equally well received.) But for the bee, blue-green is its own sublime, a pleasurable recognition simultaneous with pleasure itself. Like wanting something and also wanting to want it — the right thing felt at exactly the right time. As in yes, this is the color of the thing I most desire, as I'm sinking six legs deep into its clover-sea.

2.

Bees can't see red: they are blinded to it. What for humans is bright and violent for them is a palette of grey. Like an uncanny desire, out of nowhere — something you didn't know you could want, yet are suddenly asked to receive. Are receiving. A bite of grey cake on a rainy day pushed into the mouth: then sudden sensation of pink. And once you've tasted it — how to find that blind pleasure again? Close your complex eyes, seek with long tongue, touch your way toward the difference between a rock and a rose.

3.

What for humans is transparent to a bee is ultraviolet. When a body slips into another body — that's a feeling, not a color: transparent and raw and hardly worth looking at. But for bees it can make a pattern — efflorescence of pollination. Think of it as the clear color of change: liquid to structure, and vice versa. As a freezing day's water will vertebrae ice. As in, I am still myself, molecularly composed, but crystallized translucent by the heat of your entry.

DIONYSUS RESTORED

Do I seem drunk to you?
Apples mean night now. Torches day.
Roses still mean ultramundane happiness
and I wear them slung around my slender hips.
When you see me touch my hair, girlish gesture
of a boy you'd know anywhere, you've got it wrong –
I was gesturing for song, for double-pipes,
for power-ballad karaoke.
O ankle boots, O little cape of a great skinned cat,
its small head resting on my chest,
O ivy growing over everything,
its green breath as I lean into you
up against this wall.

TIDES RISING, ORBIT SLOWING

Angels are architecture
    without mass —
        but they move, and
with their movements
    move others
        (the planets spin
from one effortless push
    of heaven's foot).
        Meanwhile,
the whole universe
    is falling —
        falling farther apart —
even our moon
    grows more distant
        each year
(though we look up,
    look her in the face
        each day).
So our sins are blown away from us
    on invisible winds —
        we fear
without them we may
    lose ourselves altogether.
        Looking at each other,
you and I hold fast
    to our own dark matter —
        like olives to their pits —
nursing our tenuous gravities.

ADVICE FROM A WAYFARER (LAÜSTIC)

Well, I am the Captain of Fun
and my wife is a Captain too.
She wears a green onion in her hair;
her chest is heavy with medals
won from the drinking.
Whenever I see a full glass, I say,
"Drink up – this life won't last – "
making my dutiful rounds.
(Our son is a balding clown.
He hasn't any medals.
And where is his moustache
combed like a seabird in flight?)
I am the King of the Community Center!
I am pink balloons against the low ceiling!
Tip your cups! Cock your hats!
I am last year's picture
hanging on the wall!
            Though life hasn't always been so grand –
when my wife was just a girl
in a dark house across a dark wall
from mine.
            Come to the window, love.
Let us exchange possessions.
I still have it – that small vessel –
all pure gold and good stones –
the casket's still sealed
and the nightingale inside it.

REQUIRING YOUR IMMEDIATE ATTENTION

Please lift the heavy lid off the morning.

Insomnia never pays overtime
though I've worked this 3:00 A.M. shift
week after week.

FYI, some people are very sensitive
to overhead fluorescent lights
and what day is it today.

Mark on this form how many hours
expected in this month,
and of that number how many
ready to ship on demand.

Consider the cost effectiveness of breathing

and take a moment's rest beneath
the summer trees finally
caught up on their paperwork —

the beautiful green triplicates of summer
we'll separate later to save
like receipts in our books.

Our records show last year's affection
was improperly filed.

We require your immediate attention
anytime during regular business hours
Eastern Standard Time.

POSTCARD (AFTER RILKE'S ROSES)

The heart is an artichoke, am I right?
The butterflies and moths
are exiting the pages!
If you say it just that way,
releasing them one by one
from the artichoke.
Hey, I was like you, looking up love
in the dictionary like some
heliotrope of higher feeling –
until language just choked
VLKUBOOM
and the heart was handed
its electric nerve petals.

HOW CORAL IS MADE

A traffic cone up in a tree, a sure sign of spring.
At any moment I expect blossoms will extend through it,
like the feet of a barnacle
fluttering like eyelashes
beyond their carapace,
tasting the world beyond.

What's wrong with me?
I, too, have stuck my head in a dark hole
I've built of my responsibilities,
refusing the bright spring light
to finish just one more thing
all day long,
though my feelings furious fleet
like barnacle feet.
Love was once a larval-state sailor, his youthful swim.

The sea *is* complicated,
building a colony of calcified families
from the carefree polyp states.
A world our grandchildren may never see
as ocean acidic dissolves:
those *were* pearls that were his eyes
of his bones coral made.

NOCTURNE

All night the lemons fell eerily quiet
and we gathered them in our handbags
as the moon sent out one long antenna
from behind the mountain cliff.
Then the body, a mollusky white,
muscled over the craggy edge.

A strange lunar breeze picked up,
and you turned your face to it.
I couldn't hear what you said,
but your tone looked serious,
earnest in a way you rarely are —

while the celestial gastropodinal foot
rippled across the seaweed-slick dark,
escaping the ravenous stars.

EATING LIGHT BULBS FOR A LIVING

Even the sun's got a parasol
these hungover days. On the streets, roaming,
too bright, too parched, too many problems to solve.

In this town I'm unknown
as the new moon, regardless
of previous history, how many hearts overthrown —

And who calls Venus heartless?
Every planet's got its problems: we're all just trying
to get a little more for less.

I like my stars like I like my rye —
neat, with just a splash of candelabra.
There, there, it's no use crying,

I say to my friend, the empty bar stool. Abracadabra!
Make this life disappear faster than a brassiere!

IN GREAT SWARMS

My thoughts thronged a long wrong road.
My lost lover lolled an old toothpick.
The cells of the body harbor something dire – a secret
they express through slow secretion.
Will you please
quicken my breath, the turn, the door, oh goodbye
and 1, 2, 3   1, 2, 3 – the waltz skips the double heartbeat –
the creak of departure, the strain of a boat roped.
The skirt slaps the skin, the skull slams to sleep,
the sky skids past.
I am a morning sneak, a *marone*, a mortal.
I felt the sun come sniff the side of my face.
The road grew longer with each step I didn't take,
59 days of nonconsecutive stomachache.
Is this what you mean when you say I should grow up
in America
in love, in love, in love, fatal, fatal,
at night, in great swarms, as many of us would like to do?

PALINODE / ODE ON A WEDDING DAY

The bride and groom

                              Big white moon

will mend the cake,

                              flashes her belly,

reverse the dance,

                              and I'm happy and crying

and the guests will lift

                              like a fish tied with ribbons.

the gifts off the table,

carry those burdens away.

                              The radio never stops

                              playing love songs;

We can't recant

                              but we stay in the car

the song we sang —

                              just to hear the last song through.

there's evidence:

the photo album,

                              Count and recount

our mouths wide open —

                              the times you've heard this —

                    how sure we feel, how we just knew.

but we can put the records

in their sleeves, give the sleeves

                    The guests are tired,

away, drive off

                    the sun has set,

and nothing more to say.

                    tearstained bride and groom

                    refuse to leave the dance floor.

I am angry and laughing

like a gosling swallowing pearls.

                    What happens next?

                    Unbelievers – eat this cake!

And love still exists,

                    And then what happens?

thin as a motel towel.

                    Hopeless – catch this bouquet!

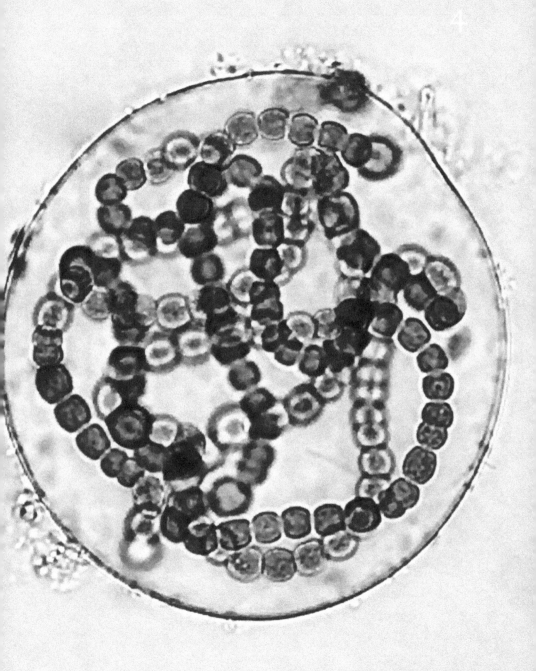

PILGRIMAGE

Pilgrim –
Awake to bells with no melody or reason.
You were given this tongue and body
and all day long your life rings you,
rings you for what you are worth,
but you can't hear it amidst the pound
of traffic, heat, and senseless shouting.

Sit down by the fountain
outside the closed church
and listen to water
diffusing into light.

All pilgrims' feet are painted black.
It is good if you've lost something –
your map, your luggage, your companions,
your favorite ring, your last coin,
your metal heart, your language.

Go to the marketplace.
Touch everything, pilgrim.
Let every cloth remind you
that you have hands.

Let your eyes go blind
on their clever toys and cheap purses.
Pay the toll to the King of Fleas,
his plastic cane rapping
on the world's refuse.

In the heap, find a book of poems
written as if in your heart's own tongue.
Did you know you were hungry as this, pilgrim,

here by the clamor of handmade wind chimes
and songbirds for a penny? Happy
as you are, despite everything,
cracking open a seed.

DAPHNE AND APOLLO

At first it's as simple as two people running.
Running from one story into another.
Another second, she'll scream out in bowers.
Bowers of new green so tender it hurts her.
Her hands become haloes that twig bone to branches.
Branches that carry her up into sunlight.
Sunlight that sinks a warm hand into belly.
Belly that gives way to rough bark and breakneck.
Breakneck the turning from fear into arbor.
Arbor for armor, his ardor outlasts her.
Her sense turns to sun-dapple, leaf-hiss, surrender.
Surrender the girl for the heartbeat worth saving.

DEATH

Mostly I don't talk to you about death.
I walk very carefully near it,
rolling from the outside of the foot in,
so you won't hear a step fall.
I wrap it round and round in batting
so any sound of it is muffled,
maybe you won't even
know I
mentioned it,
won't feel the thud of it,
or absence of thud.
Once a friend was so kind
the death in me burst into tears,
enough tears to fill my whole body.
I did not know the death in me
had been so sad about death,
or had secretly been building up
such a reservoir.
Did it ask every cell
to hold a little
while I was sleeping?
Am I wrong to be so quiet about it,
as I am about so many things?
Should I say it instead every day
like I love you,
not just on special occasions,
or only when I sense
that the other person is
likely to say it too?
Maybe when this is all over
we can sit down
and have a long talk about it.
Death must speak many languages,

including the languages of animals.
And plants too, though that is less a language
and more a network of feelings.
I am guessing it also speaks silences
like a good Swedish film
and probably also trumpets
like a New Orleans parade.
I watch death move
like a drop of black liquid
unfurling in a glass of water,
imagining itself
a new spiked green
uncurling into a leaf.
There were not any miracles today.
But it is spring.
Or the miracle is
if you are reading this
you are alive.
Let it shine, let it shine, let it shine.

VILLANELLE FOR FALSE SPRING

What goes around comes around again.
The birds think spring, and maybe I do too.
But when I listen, silence on the line.

I listen harder, hear the colors strain.
The pill is bitter, that the tulips took.
What goes around comes around again.

We're all under the weather, sky is fine.
We try to slip inside that narrow blue.
    Will a photo make it true?
Two crows land silent on the line.

All ears, all eyes, all senses at attention.
It is too much, the nerves' raw green shoots.
What goes around comes around again.

But still so cold: it's just the sun that shines.
The thought that counts, but never reaches you.
I try to write you now, a silent line.

Call it a day, whatever these hours contain.
Close the book, some things you can't un-do.
But what goes around comes around again.
Spring un-writing winter, line by line.

PARKING LOT SONNET,
OR TIMOTHY TRIES TO GIVE ME HIS NUMBER WHILE
THE LADY HE CAME WITH GROWS IMPATIENT

"Seriously, Timothy, you are breaking my heart,"
says the dolled up girl in the parking lot.
You like blondes, and she's a good start —
voluptuous and sad, thankfully not

unaccustomed to life's disappointments.
It's clear to everyone that you're a good dancer,
or, in other words, a boy who'll make rent —
borrowing, when you need it, someone else's answer.

Meanwhile, Timothy, I'm falling through the sky,
lonelier than ever. Nice to meet you. The gun's under
my pillow, burning colder by the hour. Why dance, why
begin anything, when what we take for first kiss wonder

is the first quake of the ending beneath our feet. The girl
is in the car, waiting. Get in, drive faster.

FOUR PICTURES

1.

Sitting slumped on the edge
of the neatly made bed
in the low-ceilinged motel room.

Not looking at the bureau's
framed Assurance of Quality.

Not looking at your hands
folded, sleeves rolled up.

Not even a suitcase here.
Jacket hung up neatly,
like a joke.

2.

It is easy to want
three things at once —

one choice, its opposite,
and the gentle strain between.

Now if each way had a wire,
and you the light bulb in the center.

3.

Dirt road and a rocky field
and an empty bench.

No two clouds are ever alike,
and no cloud is even like itself
one minute to the next.

"You've changed," they say
to one another.

But inside, each cloud
perceives itself
as something it once was —

small and cumulus,
gloomy and nimbus,
a monstrous bunny,
a dragon-headed snail.

4.

An ocean of wheat washes up
to the billboard horizon
of cursive Coca-Cola,

then sweeps past, off and over
the edge of the world.

A side-of-the-road snapshot
made into a postcard

from when your car broke down;
from the last time you were happy.

RETURNING TO POMPEII

People will wish on anything: an Imperial-era basin
with no magical properties other than being
out of our reach. Behind a metal fence,
its dry fountain spouts wishful coins
splashing in and around it,
next to Our Goddess of Archeological Crates
quietly arranging her scattered limbs,
and a few casts of bodies that appear to be crying
but were only trying to breathe
in the House of Mysteries.

What happened here?
A toothy mask, a pillow tied to the head,
an arm over the eyes, a spice jar opened
and then closed again.
Later they will say we believed in seagoats
and waded daily into lustral waters.
Later they will discover our voices
were only in our heads
yet easily amplified
to the back of the amphitheater.

Today you open your mouth a crack
and I pour the plaster in
to know the shape of your word,
your last gesture.

Back then red
was the color of light
and we invented walls with it.
We were always walking into fire.

NOCTURNE

Someone died in the house next door
and crossed my path as I headed down
through sodden leaves to the home I'd known
almost as long as I'd known you for.

The gurneymen, casual, not unkind,
worked quietly, and the falling night
seemed lit by the formal zippered white
gliding into the street like a slowly wheeled sun.

You were waiting on the porch – I joined you there.
We watched the form eased into an unassuming car.
You'd been angry at me but took my hand to your heart.
The engine coughed into the windless air.

And then there was nothing but trees, buildings, dark,
but we stayed till the silence had swallowed its mark.

PRIMITIVE ANIMAL, A DRIFTER IN DUST

"A man, if hard put to it, can get along quite well without talking."
— LIFE Nature Library: *Animal Behavior*

Storing grain in one of a hundred chambers.
Casting a shadow that cuts the sun's glare.

He beckons fish to the shade.
Begins to wave a claw.

A tin maze, a turtle and dish of water
provide a simple answer to a question.

He finds the chain tied to the basket, pulls the basket to him,
then swings across to the cheese shelf.

Mimicking the song was not important: *Chip-chip-chip,*
tell-tell-tell, cherry-erry-erry-erry, tissy-che-wee-ooo.

He tries to blend into his surroundings by
stretching tall and thin, holding in all his feathers,

or frightened, but hidden in weeds,
a croak swells the throat – a pale beacon.

Free swimming, transparent,
his greatest need is to be scattered,

or a drifter in dust, giving out –
the "fruiting phase" over which the "animal" glides.

Words frequently become damp and germinate;
he takes them out to dry in the sun, while

a star-shaped yellow patch around his center
attracts bees to the heart, where the pollen and nectar are.[1]

---

[1] "Since the science of animal behavior must exclude such subjective words as 'joy' from its vocabulary,
phenomena like this must await further research before they can be satisfactorily explained." — *Animal Behavior*

POSTCARD (LIKE)

It's very hard to hear Finland
from inside a styrofoam cup,
like the way you said I love you
by never saying it,
like snow on the ground,
like swearing under your breath,
like wish heard as *fisk*,
only that's Swedish
like B's mother
enjoying
with a worried brow
the fruit trees
and their too early blossoms.

The heart is a heap of small potatoes
for which we are thankful
this hard winter.

VITA NUOVA

— after the architecture of Borromini

As easy as a swarm of bees
Infesting the nook of your crazy geometry,
White on white, light lingers in the coffers.

What have you come here for?
The blessings of a saint's kerchief,
As easy as a swarm of bees,

Or to hide in a church
No bigger than a pillar,
Infesting the nook of your crazy geometry?

White bowls of water
Are left out for cats and martyrs.
White on white, light lingers,

And even the façade sways.
A wingbone encased in stone
Flutters like a saint's kerchief,

Yet here you are, still waiting.
A blessing of bees infests
The carving of a pillar,

The nook of your mind,
The empty bowl of a coffer.
A cross-section of martyr eases

White on white from pure geometry,
But you are wooden, an empty
Prayer, a hidden swarm.

HOLLYWOOD TREATMENT

— after Lydia Davis

Ten years later and again she bursts
out the same front door in the same undone raincoat
to run smack into the same perfect for her,
wrong for her, perfect for her lover
and a song and dance sequence.

They try again, they share a Coke Classic,
they share some extra long camera shots
and ten-years-later-wiser faces —
in the same café where they first met
with all the dreamy lighting
of a flashback montage,
before the sad music pipes in
to let them know
audience polls prefer
a sad ending.

(Though the women will mask their crying
with more shifting-of-popcorn noises,
and the men will brusquely guffaw
in hurt disbelief at the heart's loud
clamor and refusal.)

But wait! It's a happy ending
disguised as a sad ending
disguised as a happier ending,
and a wedding, and the bad guys,
and the good guys, and the dead mother,
and the funny neighbor, and the one more kiss,
and *Coke is it!*, and the rain falls harder,
and the war averted, and the children reunited,
and all our strength to quiet us.

THE FILM PLAYED BACKWARDS

Here on the dusty green of the old Etruscan road,
where strange red-winged bees lure you further,
the buzzing ripples like an iridescent sheen.
Farther, in a tunnel through the hill
you breathe roots, absorbing
your life, diffused Lethe: in.

Out into light again,
the city streets, a waiting lover,
all an ivy-covered world now, as a snake
lifts its head up and reverses, a tear
back to the eye.
I turned, a long time ago, hardly realizing.
I roam the Roman streets flooded with wine.

FORGIVENESS TOUR

Forgive me I was drinking with my grandfather in the cemetery
Forgive me I was writing a five-page introduction for a bag of wind
Forgive me I was reading the unpublished manuscript of the autumn leaves
Forgive me I wanted a tiny monkey to beat a tiny drum for my parade

Forgive me I was crying in sympathy with the weatherman
Forgive me I was taking lessons from the lampshade
Forgive me I was embroidering winter on my pillow
Forgive me I was giving flowers to robots

Forgive me I was "burgeoning" and "assuaging"
Forgive me I was picking out the seeds of hurt with a sterilized pin
Forgive me I was "keeping traditions alive"
Forgive me I was making the first time "special"

Forgive me I stopped for a whiskey and felt I'd fallen in love just as
    the jukebox kicked in
Forgive me that boy's halo astounded in beauty
Forgive me I was wrapping a hardcover of early lesbian fiction
    in a scarf of green silk
Forgive me I can't sleep although I am sleepy

Forgive me the teacup just fit my hand perfectly
Forgive me I was temping as a mattress factory affiliate
Forgive me I thought life could be a silent movie and the words
    would appear several frames from now of their own accord
Forgive me that almost ruined my life also

Forgive me I can't come to the phone right now but if you'd like to leave
    a message please do so after the tone
Forgive me I have not seen you in over a year
Forgive me I was singing *Blue Jay, Blue Jay*
Forgive me there is no reflection on the lake

Forgive me they were never married although they talked about it
Forgive me the ash in the air has swallowed the shadows

Forgive me we were made of wood when we made our wedding bed
Forgive me I stopped speaking because I was afraid

Forgive me the train at Montparnasse slid through the 2nd floor window
        and crashed on the Paris street
Forgive me I was swindled by a coward with a villain's moustache
Forgive me I sit alone at Table 13
Forgive me the ground began to snow back up to the sky

Forgive me there was blood on the floor but I didn't know it
Forgive me sometimes I doubt spring really will come
Forgive me I stopped dead in my tracks and the stars were cold and sharp
Forgive me I heart Harpo Marx

Forgive me I believed all the untrue things you believed about me
Forgive me I hope you never take back your green couch I really like it
Forgive me I did see a U.F.O. when I was 7
Forgive me a cosmonaut and a bathysphere go dancing

Forgive me I sometimes apologize when I myself have been hurt
Forgive me in 1997 I was sick on the future when I should have been
        laughing with glee
Forgive me that gentle breeze is swaying its antlers
Forgive me I think it will get better

Forgive me I am tap dancing for peanuts
Forgive me we are experiencing turbulence and I have returned to my seat
        and kept my seatbelt safely fastened
Forgive me a small kindness can sometimes break me
Forgive me that elephant is my daughter

Forgive me I can't take her back.
Forgive me we can't take me back.
Forgive me forward was back.
Forgive me the long way back.

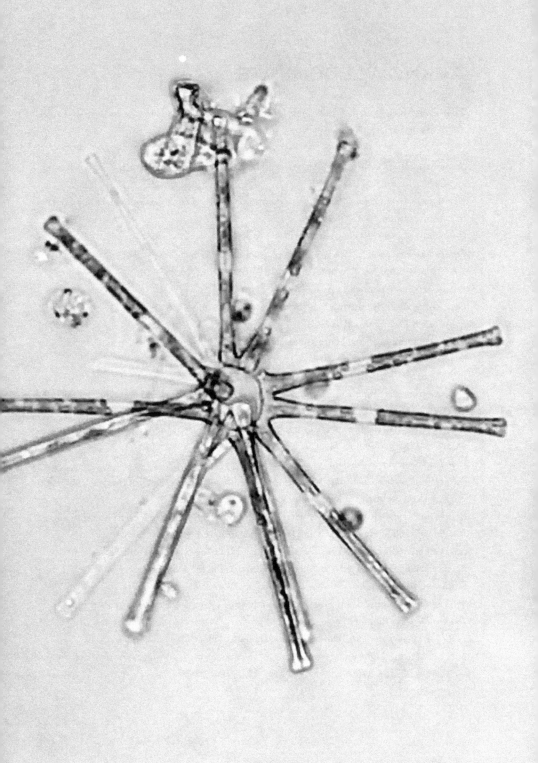

ACKNOWLEDGMENTS

Thank you to the journals and publications in which the following poems first appeared (some in variation, under previous titles):

Anthony Hecht Prize Anthology (Waywiser Press): "We Take the Funicular," "Tides Rising, Orbit Slowing"

Birmingham Arts Journal: "Palinode / Ode on a Wedding Day" (National Hackney Poetry Award winner)

City Arts Magazine: "In Great Swarms"

Cranky Literary Journal: "Four Methods of Speaking," "Advice from a Wayfarer (Laüstic)," "Almost Breakfast Anytime," "It Is Still a Beautiful Dream"

Crazyhorse: "Not Towards a Real, Towards Another"

Erg Literary Zine: "Requiring Your Immediate Attention"

Fairy Tale Review: "For LRRH"

Fou: "Detectaphone" and "Forgiveness Tour"

Los Angeles Review: "Nocturne [*There is a sound of an animal crunching*]"

Louis Liard International Journal: "Everyman and Her Chorus"

Mare Nostrum: "Daphne and Apollo," "Pilgrimage," "Vita Nuova," "Let a Little Light In"

Monarch Review: "Parking Lot Sonnet," "Four Pictures"

Pacifica Literary Review: "Destruction Island Could Be Seen in the Distance"

PageBoy: "Postcard (Ghost Meat)"

Pleiades: "Dear Sir or Madam"

Poems for Tube-snouts and Other Secrets of the Sea Anthology (for Secrets of the Sea Exhibition, Lewiston-Auburn College, Maine): "How Coral Is Made"

Poetry Northwest: "How to Remember," "We'll Always Have Carthage," "The First Photograph," "Handle Only in Darkness or in a Red Safelight"

Poetry on Buses Anthology: "Your Eyes Are Closed But You Aren't Dreaming"

Roethke Readings Anthology: "Nocturne [*Someone died in the house next door*]"

Southern California Review: "Rules for Water"

Sun's Skeleton: "Signs," "Self-Song of the Little Jug," "Get the Gods on the Aerophone"

Tahoma Review: "Pickup Truck Pantoum"

TLR (The Literary Review): "Hollywood Treatment," "Death"

Thermos: "Eating Light Bulbs for a Living," "Eyeglasses for Insomniacs, or Tests of Mentality, Readiness, and Achievement"

"Rogue Wave" and "The Lachrymose Report" were previously published in the chapbook *In Case of Loss*, *Embark* Quartet Series Vol. 7 (Toadlily Press, 2012)

"Your Eyes Are Closed But You Aren't Dreaming" was previously published in *I Take Back the Sponge Cake* (Rose Metal Press, 2012)

"Not Towards a Real, Towards Another" was reprinted in *Alive at the Center: Pacific Poetry Project Anthology* (Ooligan Press, 2013)

Thank you to Sally Warring (pondlifepondlife.com) for use of her photographs for this book. The images are of microscopic organisms found in pond samples, including cyanobacteria, green algae colonies, diatoms, and a heliozoan.

Thank you to the Poetry NW Editions team for believing in this book and for all your hard work bringing it to be. Work on this manuscript was made possible with generous support from residencies at the MacDowell Colony, Vermont Studio Center, Whiteley Center, Centrum, Catwalk, Whistlestop Barn Studio, and Seattle7Writers Sorting Room. Thank you to my colleagues and students through the years at Hugo House, Writers in the Schools (WITS), Seattle Children's Hospital, and University of Washington's Creative Writing Programs in Rome, Italy and Friday Harbor Marine Laboratories. Thank you to my mother for recognizing my first poem when I was seven and encouraging me ever after, and for modeling how poetry and art can be both everyday and save your life. Thank you to my dad (a.k.a. Correspondence Man) for instilling in me a love of postcards and for all the adventures exploring tide pools and aquariums; those early loves continue to feed the poems too. Thank you to Babci and Jimpa for your love and support. Thank you to Grandma Green and Grandma Kathryn: I wish I could show you this book in person.

LHGTI (Rebecca Hoogs, Rachel Kessler, Jason Whitmarsh, Kevin Craft): I cannot thank you deeply enough for helping me keep the faith, pen to paper, poems to manuscript. This book would not exist without your camaraderie and insight. Loren Erdrich, Rock Shop ladies and Johnny Horton: your conversations reverberate here too. Stagmoats: your dreamwork helped this book find its way to reality. Richard Kenney: astrolabe, microscope, field notes — you gave me the tools to sail by. Chris Weber and Roy August: my favorite constellation, you make each turn around the sun a better one.

NOTES

"Rogue Wave": Quotation from *The History of Herodotus* translated by George Rawlinson.

"Not Towards a Real, Towards Another": Images pulled from a variety of sources; title and "not attached to any specific existence...not attached to life" from *Hegel and the Philosophy of Right* by Dudley Knowles.

"Handle Only in Darkness or in a Red Safelight": Inspired in part by Ziggy Hanaor's *Know Your Rodent*, tips from old photography manuals, and several emotions not translatable into English.

"We'll Always Have Carthage": Inspired in part by Dido, Queen of Carthage, in Virgil's *The Aeneid*, as well as classical Greco-Roman statues of Hercules, another dubious hero figure.

"Lost & Found": Quotation from *Either/Or: A Fragment of Life* by Søren Kierkegaard, translated by Alastair Hannay; songs from Seattle's old Canterbury jukebox.

"The Story": Opening phrase, "You're telling that story again..." inspired by Susan Browne's "On Our Eleventh Anniversary" opening line.

"Cyanobacteria and the Underworld": Part 2 begins and ends with lines from *Moby Dick*; Part 3 uses phrases borrowed from the Hungarian-English Dictionary.

"Advice from a Wayfarer (Laüstic)": Inspired by "Lay of the Nightingale" by Marie de France.

"Vita Nuova": Borrows a phrase describing the architecture of Borromini, "as easy as a swarm of bees," from Eleanor Clark's *Rome and a Villa*.

"Hollywood Treatment": Inspired in part by Lydia Davis's short story "Fear."

INDEX

air: 11, 28, 35, 43, 44, 68, 74; *see also* breeze, wind

anchor: 20

angel(s): 14; (lower orders of) 33, (as architecture) 47

anger: 26; angry 56, 68

animal(s): 30, 33, 61, 69; *see also* aquatic organisms, birds, insects, mammals, reptiles, snail

answer: 27, 31, 64, 69; -ing machine 74; *see also* question

antenna(e): 7, 52

antler(s): 29, 75

aquatic organisms: barnacle 51; coral 51; cyanobacteria 35; frog 69; jellyfish (gowns) 42; mollusk 52; seagoats 67; (sea) stars: 52; *see also* fish

architecture: 12-13, 32, 47, 67, 71

asleep: 10, 32; *see also* sleep

attention: 49, 63

autumn: 74

awake: 59

balloon(s): 30, 48

bar (for drinking): 6, 53; *see also* restaurant

began: 11, 75

bells: 30, 59

belly: 9, 55, 60; bellies 34

birds: unidentified 42, 44, 63; blue jay 74; crows 37, 63; goldfinches 42; gosling 56; hawk 25; nightingale 48; pigeon (coops) 13; sea- 48; seagulls 15; song- 59, 69; swan (opposite of) 27

blessing(s): 71

blind: (sun is) 5, (with rhododendrons) 20; -s (window of) 20; -ing 37; -ed 45; – pleasure 45; – portraits 32; go – 59

blood: 7, 36, 75

blossom(s): 39, 51, 70; – beetles 7

boat(s): 17, 54; small craft advisory 14

bodily ailments: allergy (medicine) 20; eczema 16; plague 19; sciatica 16; swollen eye 36; *see also* stomachache, unwell

body: 29, 35, 45, 52, 54, 59, 61; bodies 67; no- 7; some- 30; back 17; hoof 37; hips 46; legs (six) 45; limbs (scattered) 67; (body) niche 44; vertebrae (ice) 45; *see also* antenna, antler, belly, blood, bone, brow, cell, chest, ear, eye, face, foot, fur, hair, hand, head, heart, moustache, mouth, nerve, shoulder, skin, skull, teeth, tongue, wing

(grey) 45, (wedding) 55-56, cake crumbs 7; caraway seed 36; cheese (hopeful) 69; eggs 8, night eggs through sugar wrapper 27; ghost meat 34; gingernut 7; green onion 48; jam 7; jelly (cherry) 8; lemons 52; nachos 19; oatmeal 7; olives 34, 47; orange 39; pancakes 8; peanuts 75; peas (strained) 36; pollen and nectar 69; pomegranate seeds 35; popcorn 72; potatoes (small) 70; rice (thrown) 12; roses 29; seeds (unspecified) 23; soup 7, 34; toast (extra butter) 8, (burnt) 19

foot: 9, 11, 47, 52, 61; feet 16, 51, 59, 64; -steps 18; heels 38

forgiveness: 74-75

found: 7, 19-20; 23; *see also* lost

fountain: 18, 59, 67

fragrance: smell of orange blossoms 39; fragrant green 29; honeysuckle 43

friend: 14, 23, 53, 61; boy- 26; lady he came with 64

fur: 9, 33; *see also* hair

gift(s): 27, 36, 55

glass: — key 26; cupping — 36, (crying windows) 42; *see also* eyeglasses, tableware, window

gods & goddesses: (on the aerophone) 14; (in fountain) 18; Our Goddess of Archeological Crates 67; Apollo 60; Dionysus (Bacchus) 46, 73; Venus (Aphrodite) 18, 53

ghost: 30; — meat 34

grief: 6, 29; *see also* feeling, lachrymose, sad, sorrow

gutter(s): 36, 42

hair: 9, 46, 48; -line 31; blondes 64; *see also* eyelash, fur, moustache

hand(s): 5, 14, 23, 24, 28, 32, 38, 39, 59, 60, 65, 68, 74; -ed 50; on — 10; long- 6; -bags 52, -made 59; fingers 30

happy: 23, 55, 59, 66, 72; happiness 6, 10, 46

head: 13, 17, 30, 46, 51, 67, 73; dragon-headed 66; *see also* mind, body, brow

heap: 36, 59, 70

hear: 43, 52, 55, 59, 61, 63, 70; -d 35, 55, 70

heart(s): 17, 20, 36, 50, 53, 59, 64, 68, 69, 70, 72; I — 75; -beat 10, 54, 60; -less 53

heat: 35, 39, 45, 59; -blown 44

heroes: Georgia O'Keefe 15; Harpo Marx 75

home: 12, 15, 68 ; -less 19

hope: 23, 35, 75; -d 7; -ful 35; -less 56, 65

house(s): 26, 36, 48, 68; — of Mysteries 67

insects: ants 43; bees 45, 69, 71, 73; beetles (blossom) 7; butterflies 50; caterpillar 7; moth(s) 7, 50; *see also* antenna, swarm

invisible: 39, 47; unseen 20

ink: 23, 32

insomnia: 49; insomniacs 27; can't sleep 74; *see also* awake

joke: 65; am I right? 50; *see also* laugh

joy: 15, 69; -ous strain 14

jukebox: 19, 74; *see also* music

key(s): (sound of) 7; (glass) 26; (typewriter) 31

kind: nothing of the – 8; – Regards 33; so – 61; not un- 68; -ness 75

king: (of Community Center) 48; (of Fleas) 49

kiss: 11, 64, 72; -ed 10; make out 12

lachrymose: 42; *see also* cry, feeling, tear

language(s): 45, 50, 59; animal 61, 69; death speaks 61; plant 62; Danish (*lykke*) 10; French (*conduire*) 25, (*dormir*) 10, (*nous nous aimons*) 30; Swedish (*fisk*) 70; Turkish (*şerefe*) 10; slang-ish 54; *see also* translation

laugh: 37; -ed 7, 8, 19, 31; -ing 56, 75; -ter 14; *see also* joke

leaf: 62; -hiss 60; leaves 49, 68, 74

learn: 12; -ed 11; -t 36

leave: 7, 24, 39, 56, 74

letter(s): 20, 25, 27, 31; (salutations & closings) 7, 33; *see also* communication (methods of)

light: 15, 23, 29, 31, 37, 39, 51, 59, 67, 71, 73; -ing 72; -sensitive 24; sun- 12, 28, 60; microscope – 35

light bulb(s): (100-watt tungsten) 10; (eating) 53; (you in the center) 65

light fixtures: 16; candelabra 53; light switches 14; overhead fluorescent lights 49; red safelight 10

liquid: 27, 45, 62

long(ing): 12, 15, 18, 27; -ed 14; *see also* feeling, measurement

look: 13, 17, 18, 26, 33, 47; -ed 7, 52; -ing 15, 26, 45, 47, 50; – casual 6; not looking 65

lost: 7, 8, 14, 19, 20, 27, 29, 54, 59; without loss 27

love: 6, 15, 19, 20, 27, 28, 39, 42, 44, 45, 48, 50, 51, 56, 61, 70, 74; -liest 27; – letters (creepy) 25; – songs 55; *Whole Lotta Love* 19

lover(s): 16, 54, 72, 73

luck: 35

luggage: 59; bag 74; handbags 52; suitcase 65

machine(s): (dishwashing) 30; (speeding up of) 36; (answering) 74; *see also* robots

mammals: bat 6, 38; beaver 10; boars 12; cats 71; deer 29; dog 19, 32; dormouse 10; elephant 75; fur (ambiguous) 9, 33; horses 14, 37; humans 6, 15, 45; lamb 33; lion 17,

33; mice 7; monkey 74; rat 69; wolf 9; *see also* animal

map: 59

measurements: circumference (of thirst) 11; distance (can be seen in the) 15, (grows more distant) 47; drop (one too much) 36; gravities (tenuous) 47; height of genius 19; lengths (extremely long) 10; mass (zero) but with velocity 47; miles (every few) 25; watt (100) 10; weight (smoky) 34; *see also* time (measured)

metal: (barbs) 19, (coffin) 36, (fence) 67, (heart) 59; gold (pure) 48; pewter 24; silver 19, 26; tin 69; *see also* mineral

microscope: 35-36; microscopic organisms 35-36, 69

mind: 11, 18, 71; *see also* head

mineral: bitumen (of Judea) 24; chalk 31; crystal 7, 23, crystallized 45; iron 36; plaster (gypsum crystals) 67; salt 24, 36, saline 25; tufa 12; *see also* metal, rock, stone

miracle(s): 62; not any – 62

mirror: 26, 31, 36

moon: 7, 16, 19, 23, 32, 47, 52, 53, 55

mountain: 12, 19, 35, 52

morning: 28, 49, 54; *see also* time (of day)

mouth(s): 6, 9, 16, 19, 45, 55, 67; -ful 36; lip(s) 11, 31, lipped 29, lipping 29; *see also* body, teeth, tongue

moustache: 48, 75

motel: 65, – towel 56

music: (sad soundtrack) 72; accordion 12; (bands & songs): *Just My Imagination* (The Temptations) 19, Van Halen 20, *Whole Lotta Love* (Led Zeppelin) 19; birdsong (clamor) 59, (transcribed) 69; choir (divided) 36; drum (tiny) 74; joyous strain 14; karaoke (power-ballad) 46; radio 25, 55; records 56; trumpets 62; wind chimes 59; *see also* bells, communication (methods of), jukebox, sing, song

name(s): 6, 20, 33, 37, 38

nerve(s): 16 50, 63

night: 6, 7, 12, 16, 27, 35, 37, 46, 52, 54, 68; good-39; mid- 16; *see also* nocturne, time (of day)

no: 7, 16, 19, 23, 27, 35, 36, 59, 65, 67, 71, 74; -body 7; -where 45; – longer 18; – need 9; – one: 18; – use 14, 53; – way 14

nothing: 8, 23, 30, 34, 56, 68

nocturne: 16, 30, 52, 68; *see also* night

O: 46

Oh: (goodbye) 54

ocean: 51, 66; *see also* sea

page(s): 31, 32, 38, 50; five-page introduction 74; *see also* book

pantoum: 29

paper: 12, 29

paperwork: 49; receipts 49; records 49; report 6, 42

parade: 62, 74

pen: 32, 38; -manship 6; *see also* communication (methods of), ink

person: 28, 30, 35, 43, 61

philosophers: birds (crying in trees) 42; Hegel 7; Herodotus 6; Kierkegaard 19; little jug 11; Pascal 27; Wittgenstein 19; *see also* theory

phone: 74; aero- 14, detecta- 28; tele- 31; — line 30; *see also* communication (methods of)

photograph: 10, 24, 39; photo 63; photo album 55; snapshot 66

picture: 18, 48, 65

pillow: 64, 67, 74

places: America 54; Carthage 17; Destruction Island 15; Finland 70; France 24; Hollywood 72; Italy 18, 44, 59, 71, 73; New Orleans 62; New York 19, 26, New York City 26, Pompeii 67; Poughkeepsie 26; Turkey 15; Vancouver (B.C.) 26; beach 32; city 13, 32, 42; coastal 25; community center 48; desert 18; field(s) 25, 65; flea market 59; forest 26; (office) 49; meadow 9, 14; parking lot 64; universe 47; *see also* bar, discotheque, factory, fountain, house, motel, mountain, planet, restaurant, road, sea, tunnel, underworld

plant(s): (general) 16, 62; apple(s) 9, 31, 46; artichoke 50; clover-sea 45; flowers 9, 15, 18, 74; green shoots 63; ivy 43, (-covered world) 73; honeysuckle 43; olives 34, 47; pine needle(s) 43; poppy 43; potted plant 28; rose(s) 29, 45, 46, 50; seaweed 52; seed(s) 23, 35, 36, 43, 59, 74; tree(s) unspecified 42, 49, 51, 68, cherry tree 42, fruit frees 70, laurel tree (a.k.a. Daphne) 60, orange tree 39, walnut tree 37; wheat (ocean of) 66; tulips 63; *see also* blossom, branch, food, leaf

planet(s): 47, 53

poem(s): 7, 59; line (written) 63; *see also* book, communication (methods of)

postcard: 8, 34, 35, 50, 66, 70; *see also* communication (methods of)

prayer: 71

queen: Dido (Queen of Carthage) 17; Persephone (Queen of Hell) 35-36

question: 31, 69; (?) 7, 8, 12, 14, 17, 19, 23, 24, 25, 27, 29, 30, 32, 39, 44, 45, 46, 48, 50, 51, 53, 54, 56, 59, 61, 63, 67, 71; *see also* answer

rain: 30, 72; -y 45; -coat 72

reptiles: lizards 44; snake 73; turtle 69

remember: 16, 39; memory 19, 39

research: 19, 69

restaurant: 8, 15, 75; *see also* bar

ribbon(s): (of ants) 43, (fish tied with) 55

right: — now 74; — thing 45; — time 45; — word 29; am I — ? 50; I'm — 17

road(s): 25, 54, 65, 73; side-of-the — 66

robots: 74

rock(s): 17, 43, 44, 45; -y 65; *see also* mineral, stone

sad: 20, 61, 64, 72; -ness 15; -eyed 7; *see also* feeling, grief, lachrymose, sorrow

sail: 36, 37; -ing 5

sailor(s): 35, 51; wayfarer 48

saints & martyrs: 37, 71

science: 35, 45, 51, 69

sea: 17, 51; -weed 52; clover- 45; *see also* aquatic organisms, birds, ocean

shadow(s): 9, 24, 69, 74

shoulder(s): 11, 12, 37

sing: 11; -ing 7; (you should, out loud:) *Yer gonna lose a good thing* 7, *Blue Jay Blue Jay* 74; whistling 9; *see also* song

skin: 33, 54; lion's — 17; -ned cat 46

skull: 35, 54

sky: 15, 54, 63, 64, 75

sleep: 10, 16, 54, 74; (in feet) 16; -ing 19, 61; -y 13, 39, 74; *dormir* 10; *see also* asleep, insomnia

slip(s): 45, 63; -ped 19, 30

snail: 43, (dragon-headed) 66; mollusk 52

snow: 28, 70, 75

song: 12, 32, 46, 55, 69, 72; Self-Song 11; -birds 59; *see also* bells, communication (methods of), music, sing

sonnet: 8, 53, 64, 68

sorrow: 20, 23; *see also* feeling, grief, lachrymose, sad

speak(s): 12, 30, 61, 62; -ing 31, 75; say(s) 12, 14, 15, 27, 20 , 32, 34, 48, 50, 53, 54, 56, 61, 64, 66, 67; -ing 70 ; said 8, 9, 17, 19, 24, 30, 52, 70; unsaid 9; *see also* communication (methods of), tell

spring: 16, 51, 62, 63, 75; May 14

stomachache: 20, 54; *see also* bodily ailments, unwell

stone(s): 9, 18, 24, 25, 36, 48, 71; mad- 7; cobble- 12; *see also* mineral, rock

summer: 18, 26, 49

sun: 5, 13, 17, 24, 28, 42, 53, 54, 56, 63, 68, 69; -beam 42; -dapple 60; -light 12, 28, 60; -rise 25

surprise: 15, 34; *see also* feeling

star(s): 11, 15, 23, 52, 53, 75; -shaped 69

swarm(s): 54, 71; *see also* insects

table: 55, 75

tableware: bowl 34, 71; cups 48, styrofoam cup 70, teacup 74; dish 69; glass (drinking) 32,
   48, 62; jug 11; knife 10; plate 8, (pewter) 24; platter (giant, painted with lemons) 12;
   spice jar 67; spoon 34, 36

tear(s): 36, 42, 61, 73; -stained 56; *see also* cry, lachrymose

tell: 6, 7, 14, 27; -ing 14, 26; tell-tell-tell 69; told 30; *see also* communication (methods of),
   speak

teeth: 9; toothy 67; toothpick 54

test(s): 24, 26, 27, 69

theory (love): 17, 19, 42

throat(s): 37, 69; *see also* body, communication (methods of), sing

time: − after − 46; -s (repeated) 31, (you've heard this) 55; at -s 7; Eastern Standard Time
   49; first − 74; it's − 14; last − (you saw her) 18, (you were happy) 66; long − ago 73;
   over- 49; right − 45; this − 7; there was a − 14; took me a long − 29

time (measured): second 60; minutes 30; hours 24, 49, 63, 64; days 20, 34, 45, 46, 47, 49,
   51, 53, 54, 55, 59, 61, 63; week 49; month 49; years 6, 20, 23, 26, 27, 31, 37, 47, 48,
   49, 72, 74; 1600 27, 1939 7, 1967 27, 1993 19, 1997 75; decade (10 years later) 72;
   centuries 24; (thousands of years) 37; lifetime (dormouse) 10, (human) 9, 11, 13, 10,
   15, 37, 48, 53, 59, 73, 74, (goddess) 35; almost as long as I'd known you 68; back then
   (before Vesuvius erupted) 67; (before Adam named animals) 33; before Herodotus 6;
   orbit 6, 47; pomegranate seeds 35; *see also* time, time (of day), today

time (of day): 3:00 a.m. 49; afternoons 12; before midnight 16; business hours E.S.T. 49;
   now 10, 15, 17, 18, 23, 29, 30, 37, 46, 63, 65, 73, 74, 75; sunrise 25;
   see also morning, night

today: 49, 62, 67

tongue: 45, 59

touch: 5, 45, 46, 59; -ing 7

transparent 24, 45, 69; translucent 45

translation: (under microscope) 36; (environmental punctuation) 25; (ghost) 30; (of saints'
   bones) 37; untranslatable 27, 30, 50; untranslatable emotions 10; *see also* language

transportation (methods of): airplane 75; airport 20; basket tied to chain 69; bathysphere
   75; bus 7, 17; bus stop 6; car 20, 25, 55, 56, 64, 66, 68; funicular 12; gurney 68; train
   13, 26, 34, 75; truck 16, 29; wind chariot 27

true: 10, 19, 39, 63; un- 75

tunnel: 43, 73

upside down: 6, 24

underworld: 35, 44; Lethe 73; Persephone 35

unwell: 5; sick 75; *see also* bodily ailments, stomachache

villanelle: 63
vision: 18, 37, 45
voice(s): 20, 43, 67; *see also* communication (methods of), sing

wall(s): 17, 18, 43, 44, 46, 48, 67
wave(s): 6, 25, 39, 69
water(s): 8, 15, 18, 23, 25, 35, 45, 59, 62, 67, 69, 71; under- 17
wear (things to): armor 60; boot 36, ankle boots 46; brassiere 53; cape 46; cloak 9; dress
    (pale, summer green) 18; gown (jellyfish) 42; hems (rising) 19; hat(s) 7, 48; hood
    9; shoes (bad) 12; skirt 54; T-shirt 32; underwear (box of) 20; accessories: collars
    (crystal-studded) 7, earring (lost to moon) 19, green onion (in hair) 48, handbags (filled
    with lemons) 52, helmet 37, kerchief (saint's) 71, medals (on chest) 48, parasol 53,
    roses (around hips) 46; watch (wrist) 8; wreaths (for head) 15; *see also* coat, eyeglasses,
    moustache
wedding: 15, 55-56, 72, 75; rice in the cobblestones 12; never married 74
well (for water): 16, 23
wind(s): 17, 47; – chariot 27; – chimes 59; bag of – 74; -less 68; gale 86; *see also* breeze
window(s): 15, 20, 24, 42, 48; -sill 24
wing(s): 14, 37, 38; -bone 71; bat-wing-like 6; red-winged 73; *see also* feather
winter: 28, 63, 70, 74; wintir 27
wood: 19, 75; -en 10, 71; Holly- 72
word(s): 7, 15, 18, 19, 29, 32, 64, 67, 69, 74; *see also* communication (methods of),
    language
worry: 43; worried 70
wreck: 6; ship- 5, 20, 35; train- 75
write: 27, 63; -ing 74; cursive 66; logographers 9; longhand 6; perfect sobbing penmanship
    6; typewriter 31, typists 33; unwriting 63; *see also* book, letter, page, pen, postcard
wrong: 6, 17, 25, 29, 46, 51, 54, 61, 72; wrong wrong wrong wrong wrong 30

yes: 5, 26, 43
you: 5-10, 12-15, 17-20, 23-28, 30-34, 36-39, 42-50, 52, 54-55, 59, 61-68, 70-71, 73-75

ABOUT THE AUTHOR

Sierra Nelson was awarded the Carolyn Kizer Prize from *Poetry Northwest* in 2014. Her previous books include the chapbook *In Case of Loss* (Toadlily Press), and lyrical choose-your-own-adventure *I Take Back the Sponge Cake* (Rose Metal Press). She teaches creative writing at the Richard Hugo House, Centrum, Seattle Children's Hospital through Writers in the Schools (WITS), and the University of Washington's Friday Harbor Laboratories and Summer Writers in Rome programs. Nelson is also a founding member of the performance collaborations

The Typing Explosion and Vis-à-Vis Society, and president of Seattle's Cephalopod Appreciation Society.

The poems are set in Perpetua
Book design by Christian Larson
Printed on archival quality paper

Poetry NW Editions is an independent,
non-profit publisher of poetry in residence
at Everett Community College. This
book, the first in the Possession Sound
Poetry Series, was produced by many
hands. The inaugural editorial team
includes Kevin Craft, Katharine Ogle,
Michelle Hope Anderson, Rachel Hill,
and Victoria Wettmarshausen

CPSIA information can be obtained
at www.ICGtesting.com
Printed in the USA
LVHW092347090419
613595LV00003B/31/P